Miss Eddie's Garden

by Juan Delgado
illustrated by Sally Vitsky

 HOUGHTON MIFFLIN   BOSTON

Printed in China

ISBN 10: 0-618-88577-3
ISBN 13: 978-0-618-88577-0

23456789 SDP 16 15 14 13 12 11 10 09 08

Miss Bumble loves her garden.
She tends her plants with care.
The animals love her garden too.

18 tomato plants all in rows.
Woodchucks come running.
They take 9 tomato plants.

How many tomato plants are left?

Crows come flying.
They take 6 lettuce plants.
That leaves 9 plants.

How many lettuce plants were there before?

Miss Bumble digs up 20 carrots.
Rabbits come hopping.
They take 6 carrots.

How many carrots are left?

Foxes come trotting.

9 ears of corn disappear.

That leaves 9 ears of corn.

How many ears of corn were there before?

Miss Bumble shakes her head.
Next year, she will plant more.
Then the animals can share.

Lettuce Grows, Lettuce Goes

Draw

Visualize Look at page 4. Draw the crows you see. Draw the lettuce plant each crow is carrying.

Tell About

Look at page 4. Tell how many lettuce heads Miss Bumble planted. Tell how many plants the crows have.

Write

Look at page 4. Write about how many heads of lettuce Miss Bumble has left.